# *Drink*
# WHISKEY

### A COLLECTION OF BOURBON, RYE, AND SCOTCH WHISKY COCKTAILS

## WHALEN
### BOOK·WORKS

Kennebunkport, Maine

"Too much of anything is bad, but too much good whiskey is barely enough."

—*Mark Twain*

# CONTENTS

Introduction . . . . . . . . . . . . . . . . . . . . . . . . . . 6

Whiskey and Scotch Whisky . . . . . . . . . . . 10

Bourbon . . . . . . . . . . . . . . . . . . . . . . . . . . 86

Rye . . . . . . . . . . . . . . . . . . . . . . . . . . . . . 188

Sweeter Stuff:
Whiskey Liqueurs and Creams . . . . . . . . . 222

Index . . . . . . . . . . . . . . . . . . . . . . . . . . . 254

# INTRODUCTION

Though every type and label of whiskey has its own distinct and nuanced flavor profile, it can generally be said that whiskey is a bold and complex spirit. It has a presence all its own, and shouldn't be thrown carelessly into just any mixed drink. This is not to say that whiskey can't be versatile, but that any good whiskey cocktail should be thoughtfully built, with ingredients that balance and complement the whiskey.

Within these pages you'll find all manner of cocktails, whether you are looking for something tart and refreshing, or something darker with a little more moxie.

Of course, there are certainly those who maintain that whiskey is best served neat or on the rocks. Yet whiskey cocktails have been around since the cocktail's invention, and rank among the most iconic of old-school drinks—the aptly-named Old-Fashioned, the Manhattan, the Sazerac, the Mint Julep, and the Boulevardier, to name a few. The origins of these legendary drinks are almost as storied as the history of whiskey itself.

The earliest incarnations of the cocktail date back to the early 1800s, and for the most part were relatively straightforward combinations of alcohol, bitters, sugar, and water. Many of the whiskey cocktails that have since become tried-and-true classics follow that exact formula. What's more, the recent revival of interest in classic cocktail culture has seen all kinds of innovative bitters, shrubs, and syrups come on the scene.

In this book we've got everything from the quintessential whiskey cocktails to adventurous new creations. Many of them have been crafted either by or for the very distilleries behind our favorite whiskeys, including Jack Daniel's, Corsair, Hartfield & Co., Maker's Mark, Jim Beam, Willett, and Buffalo Trace, ensuring that they are expertly tailored to suit the label used in the recipe.

What whiskey will not cure, there is no cure for.

—*Irish Proverb*

# WHISKEY AND SCOTCH WHISKY

By its loosest definition, whiskey is any spirit distilled from grain—usually from a "mash bill" of corn, rye, wheat, malted barley, or a combination thereof. Within this loose category, there are numerous varieties of whiskey—Scotch, Tennessee whiskey, bourbon, rye, and Irish whiskey, to name but a few. Each of these is distinguished by differences in their distillation process or the makeup of their mash bill, or both. Technically, this chapter could encompass just about every drink in this book, and the cocktails within are certainly something of a mix.

Many of the following cocktails are made with American whiskeys, including the most famous Tennessee whiskey on the planet, Jack Daniel's. Tennessee whiskey shares a similar mash bill and distillation method with bourbon (see page 86), its Kentucky cousin. However, Tennessee whiskey undergoes an additional "mellowing" known as the Lincoln County Process, where the unaged whiskey is slowly filtered through charcoal to give it a smoother flavor.

In this chapter, we also have a number of drinks made with American whiskey's progenitors, the age-old malt whiskies of Scotland and Ireland, as well as some more unconventional spirits, like Corsair's Quinoa and Triple Smoke whiskeys.

The cocktails to follow run the gamut from smoky and complex to fresh and fruity, with plenty of new twists on time-honored classics along the way.

# INNUENDO

*Corsair's complex Triple Smoke Whiskey blends beautifully with the tea and fruit flavors in this cocktail. A perfect drink for anyone who enjoys a cup of Lapsang souchong.*

*—courtesy of Corsair Distillery*

---

**2 oz Corsair Triple Smoke American Whiskey**

**1 oz tea**

**³/₄ oz peach simple syrup***

**¹/₄ oz lemon juice**

**Lemon peel, for garnish**

Shake whiskey, tea, peach simple syrup, and lemon juice, and strain into a rocks glass or tall jar with ice. Garnish with a lemon peel. *Makes 1.*

*\*To make your own peach simple syrup, simply put equal parts frozen peaches, water, and sugar in a saucepan over high heat, whisking until sugar is dissolved. Remove from heat and let steep for 1 hour, then discard peaches and use or bottle syrup. Store it, refrigerated, for up to 2 weeks.*

# WHISKEY SLING

*This drink takes its inspiration from the Singapore Sling, a gin cocktail developed at the Raffles Hotel in Singapore at the turn of the century.*

*—courtesy of Jack Daniel's*

---

4 parts Gentleman Jack
Tennessee Whiskey

1 part lemon juice

1½ part simple syrup

2 dashes orange bitters

Lemon wheel, for garnish

Shake whiskey, lemon juice, simple syrup, and orange bitters with ice. Then strain into an ice-filled glass. Garnish with a lemon wheel. *Makes 1.*

# SOUTH OF NY SOUR

*A Southern spin on the Whiskey Sour, this fantastic creation from Corsair has just the right amount of spice.*

*—courtesy of Corsair Distillery*

---

2 oz Corsair Triple Smoke American Whiskey

1 oz lemon

1 oz simple syrup

Egg white

5 drops BBQ bitters

1 oz malbec

Cracked pink peppercorns

Combine whiskey, lemon, simple syrup, egg white, and bitters in a mixing tin without ice and shake to froth egg. Add ice and shake again. Strain into a rocks glass with fresh ice. Top up with malbec. Garnish with cracked pink peppercorns. *Makes 1.*

# JACK & COLA

*An all-time classic, this iconic pairing of flavors has inspired a slew of culinary inventions, from barbecue sauces to popsicles.*

*—courtesy of Jack Daniel's*

---

**1 part Jack Daniel's Old No. 7 Tennessee Whiskey**

**3 parts cola**

**Slice of lime, for garnish**

Build whiskey and cola over ice in a tall glass, garnish with slice of lime. *Makes 1.*

# WHISKEY NUT

*If you're from the South, chances are you've dropped a handful of peanuts into your cola before. Why this is just a southern tradition is a mystery; people everywhere are well aware of the delicious combo that is sugar and salt. The Whiskey Nut takes the sweet and salty partnership and adds a dose of whiskey and orange to give you something new and impressive to show off.*

—Shane Carley

2 oz whiskey

1 dash orange liqueur

2 drops peanut extract

6 oz cola

1 orange wheel, for garnish

1 handful peanuts, for garnish

(1) Fill a rocks glass or Mason jar halfway with ice and add whiskey and orange liqueur (just enough to taste).

(2) Add peanut extract and top up with cola.

(3) Garnish with an orange wheel and a handful of peanuts. You can either eat them on the side or pop them right into the glass like you would with a can of cola! *Makes 1.*

# JACK & GINGER

*The fresh, sweet, and slightly spicy flavor of ginger ale is always a great companion to Tennessee Whiskey.*

*—courtesy of Jack Daniel's*

---

1 part Jack Daniel's Old
No. 7 Tennessee Whiskey

3 parts ginger ale

1 lemon or lime slice, for garnish

Build whiskey and ginger ale over ice. Garnish with lemon or lime slice. *Makes 1.*

# JACK DANIEL'S DISTILLERY

*By Carlo DeVito*

Jack Daniel's, located in Lynchburg, Tennessee, is the best-selling whiskey in the world—moving even more product than Johnnie Walker, who it recently surpassed.

Jasper Newton "Jack" Daniel, born in 1850, was of Irish, Scottish, and Welsh descent. The youngest of 10 children, he learned how to make whiskey in the 1850s from Reverend Dan Call and Call's slave and distiller, Nathan "Nearest" Green. Green became a mentor to Jack Daniel, and was instrumental in helping him develop his whiskey. In 1875, Daniel and Call established a distillery. Now a free man, Green was hired as its head distiller. By 1884, Daniel owned the company outright and purchased the land where the distillery now resides.

Daniel died in Lynchburg on October 10, 1911. While there is an apocryphal tale that his death resulted from an infection that sprouted after he kicked the safe in his office, this is not true. He died of blood poisoning. His nephew, Lemuel "Lem" Motlow, ran Jack Daniel's for the next 36 years and built it into one of the biggest brands in the country. The company was sold to the Brown-Forman Corporation in 1956, and at last made it onto the National Register of Historic Places in 1972.

The current distillery is a truly massive operation. Jack Daniel's has six constantly working stills, four column stills and two pot stills, all of which are 100% copper. The distillery also has its very own burn station where the charcoal for the "mellowing process" is made in a carefully controlled setting. It is only once the spirit is slowly filtered through charcoal tanks that it becomes Tennessee whiskey. The distillery fills roughly 2,000 barrels of whiskey a day, which will age in one of the 89 rickhouses throughout Lynchburg.

## FACT:

One-third of all Scotch whisky is aged in former Jack Daniel's barrels.

# TENNESSEE MULE

*If you prefer a spicier ginger beer to ginger ale, this is your drink. At once warming and refreshing, the Tennessee Mule is a cocktail for all seasons.*

*—courtesy of Jack Daniel's*

1 part Jack Daniel's Old
No. 7 Tennessee Whiskey

1 squeeze of fresh lime juice

3 parts ginger beer

Lime wheel, for garnish

Mint, for garnish

In a copper mug filled with ice, stir to combine whiskey, lime juice, and ginger beer, and serve over ice. Garnish with a lime wheel and sprig of mint. *Makes 1.*

# IRISH ROSE

*It's a bit unusual to see Irish whiskey paired with fruity mixers, but the Irish Rose defies convention. This cocktail is sure to dazzle at any gathering, and is the perfect choice to give your guests something new and exciting.*

*—Shane Carley*

---

**2 parts Irish whiskey**

**3 parts lemon-lime soda**

**1 lime wedge, juiced**

**1 lemon wedge, juiced, plus another to garnish**

**1 part grenadine**

(1) Put ice in a rocks glass. Add whiskey and lemon-lime soda.

(2) Squeeze the juice of one lime wedge and one lemon wedge into the drink, then top with grenadine. Stir until thoroughly mixed.

(3) Garnish with another lime wedge and enjoy! *Makes 1.*

# CACTUS JACK

*A tart, fruity cocktail you can sip on-the-go or on-the-sly.*
*—created by Paul Knorr*

---

**1 part whiskey**
**1 part pineapple vodka**
**1 part orange juice**

Shake whiskey, pineapple vodka, and orange juice with ice and strain into a rocks glass or pour into your flask using a funnel. *Makes 1.*

# BELLINI

*The Bellini was originally created by Giuseppe Cipriani, founder of the famed Harry's Bar in Venice, Italy. Frequented by stars and luminaries such as Ernest Hemingway, Truman Capote, and Aristotle Onassis, Harry's Bar was the epitome of café society glamour, which this drink certainly evokes. This incarnation of the Bellini gets an added kick of Gentleman Jack.*

*—courtesy of Jack Daniel's*

---

**1 part Gentleman Jack Tennessee Whiskey**

**1 part peach purée**

**Champagne**

Combine peach purée and Gentleman Jack in a glass. Top up with champagne. *Makes 1.*

# BROWN DERBY

*Let's take things to a classy place with the Brown Derby, a classic whiskey cocktail that doesn't try too hard to overwhelm you with complex flavors. Made with grapefruit juice, whiskey, and honey, this simple and refreshing cocktail proves that when it comes to ingredients, less is often more. The Brown Derby allows the sweet grapefruit juice to play off the whiskey, dulling the sharp edge of the grapefruit flavor only slightly with the addition of a spoonful of honey.*

*—Shane Carley*

---

2 oz maple whiskey

2 oz grapefruit juice

½ oz honey

Grapefruit slice, for garnish

(1) Fill a cocktail shaker with ice and add maple whiskey, grapefruit juice, and honey. Shake vigorously until thoroughly mixed.

(2) Add ice to your glass and strain the cocktail shaker into it.

(3) Garnish with a slice of grapefruit (leave the rind on) and enjoy! *Makes 1.*

# JACK JULEP

*Jack Daniel's riff on the traditional Mint Julep swaps out bourbon for charcoal-mellowed Tennessee whiskey.*

—*courtesy of Jack Daniel's*

2 parts Jack Daniel's Old
No. 7 Tennessee Whiskey

1 pinch sugar

1 mint sprig, plus a leaf to garnish

Crushed ice

Shake whiskey, sugar, and mint vigorously with ice cubes. Strain into a double old-fashioned glass full of crushed ice and garnish with a mint leaf. *Makes 1.*

# RENEGADE LEMONADE

*It's a simple recipe, but sometimes the simplest drinks are the most satisfying. You'll quickly find yourself going back for seconds.*

—Shane Carley

---

1 cup simple syrup

Juice of 6 lemons

1 cup whiskey

4 cups cold water

1 mint sprig, for garnish

2 or 3 lemon wheels, for garnish

(1) Add ice to a half-gallon pitcher and add the simple syrup, lemon juice, and whiskey, then top up with water. Stir until thoroughly mixed.

(2) Pour into four Mason jars and garnish with sprigs of mint and a few lemon wheels both inside and outside the jars. *Makes 4.*

# APPLE SANGRIA

*Full of crisp autumnal flavors, this take on sangria is perfect for raising a glass to the changing seasons.*

*—courtesy of Jack Daniel's*

---

4 parts chardonnay (low-oak)

²/₃ parts Jack Daniel's Single Barrel

¹/₃ parts apple brandy

1¹/₂ parts pure apple cider

¹/₃ parts honey

Sliced ginger

Cinnamon sticks

Apple slices

Lemon slices

Juice of 1 lime

Juice of 1 lemon

In a pitcher, combine chardonnay, whiskey, apple brandy, apple cider, honey, ginger, and cinnamon sticks; refrigerate. Before serving, add apple slices and citrus and mix well. *Makes 1.*

# BLACK FOREST

*A decidedly grown-up drink, the Black Forest complements the Triple Smoke with Hünerkopf Alt, a rich German half-bitter with aromas of orange rind, allspice, and brandied cherries.*

—*courtesy of Corsair Distillery*

---

**2 oz Corsair Triple Smoke American Whiskey**

**½ oz Hünerkopf Alt "German Half Bitter"**

**¼ oz sorghum syrup (2:1 sorghum to water)**

**Pinch of salt**

**Lemon twist, for garnish**

Stir whiskey, bitters, sorghum syrup, and salt in a mixing glass with ice. Strain into a snifter. Garnish with lemon twist. *Makes 1.*

# DARK SIDE

*This original creation from the minds at Hartfield & Co. balances the rich flavors of whiskey and Bonal with a one-two citrus punch of lime juice and orange bitters.*

*—courtesy of Hartfield & Co.*

2 oz Hartfield & Co. American Whiskey

³/₄ oz simple syrup
(1:1 sugar to water)

1 oz Bonal

³/₄ oz fresh lime juice

7 dashes Regan's orange bitters

1 lime wheel, for garnish

Build whiskey, simple syrup, Bonal, lime juice, and orange bitters in a shaker, add ice, and shake. Double strain into Collins glass over fresh ice. Top with lime wheel and serve. *Makes 1.*

# HARTFIELD & CO. DISTILLERY

*By Carlo DeVito*

It's impossible not to fall in love with Hartfield & Co. This incredibly cool yet entirely unpretentious distillery is located in Paris, Kentucky. Nestled in the heart of Bourbon Country, they are the first, and so far only, distiller of bourbon since 1911!

Founded by Andrew Buchanan and his wife Larissa in 2014, the brand is named for one of Andrew's ancestors, who also distilled bourbon in Bourbon County before Prohibition wiped out the industry. Their distillery is located in an old, turn-of-the-century feed building from 1911 that was a Chevrolet dealership in the 1920s and later an antiques warehouse. The tasting room is studded with old, late 19th century pharmacy counters and display cabinets, and the whiskey is packaged in old-fashioned apothecary bottles with labels that look like something from an ancient pharmacy.

Assisted by Jeremy Coffey, the Hartfield & Co. team lets the beer ferment longer than most distillers, as they strive to bring out the brandy, cognac, apple, and pear notes in their product. Their goal is not to let the wood overpower their spirits, but rather have the wood complement it. Each small batch is aged in small, five-gallon American oak barrels. They use Minnesota oak, which Andrew will tell you is sugar rich. These small barrels allow more liquid-to-wood contact, and thus whiskey can thus be pushed out faster. But here is where Hartfield differs from the world. They don't want their whiskey to be in the wood too long. It all sounds a bit screwy, but the proof of their philosophy is in the glass.

It sounds like mere marketing until you actually taste the whiskeys.

With an impressive lineup that includes bourbon, wheated bourbon, rum, and the most flavorful and impactful white whiskey around, this is small batch craft distilling at its best. Hartfield is the real thing. Given the quality of the spirit, the beauty of the design, and their upstart sentiment, it is hard not to root for them. If they can hold on and keep their heads about them, Hartfield & Co. are sure to be around for generations to come.

# SNAKE BITE

*Between the sharpness of the tart lime juice and hefty kick of whisky, its easy to see how this cocktail got its name.*

*—created by Paul Knorr*

---

**4 parts Canadian whisky**

**1 part fresh lime juice**

Shake whisky and lime juice with ice and strain into a glass or pour into your flask using a funnel. *Makes 1.*

# SINGLE BARREL OLD-FASHIONED

*Jack Daniel's robust Single Barrel Select Tennessee Whiskey elevates this classic cocktail.*

—*courtesy of Jack Daniel's*

---

2 parts Jack Daniel's Single Barrel Select Tennessee Whiskey

³/₄ parts simple syrup

Orange slice

Couple dashes of bitters

Maraschino cherry, for garnish

Put whiskey, simple syrup, orange slice, and bitters in a rocks glass. Muddle the orange. Add ice and stir. Garnish with a cherry. *Makes 1.*

# OLD AS DIRT

*This excellent riff on the Old-Fashioned uses Corsair Quinoa Whiskey, one of the distillery's signature madcap inventions.*

*—courtesy of Corsair Distillery*

---

**2 oz Corsair Quinoa Whiskey**

**½ oz honey simple syrup**

**Old-Fashioned bitters**

**Orange twist, for garnish**

Combine whiskey, honey simple syrup, and bitters in a rocks glass with ice and stir. Garnish with orange twist. *Makes 1.*

# JACK DANIEL'S BOULEVARDIER

*The bittersweet Boulevardier dates back to the 1920s and first appeared in print in 1927, in the Harry's New York Bar in Paris manual, Barflies and Cocktails. Its invention is attributed to American writer and socialite Erskine Gwynne, who ran the literary magazine Boulevardier.*

*—courtesy of Jack Daniel's*

---

**1¹/₂ oz Jack Daniel's Single Barrel Proof**

**¹/₂ oz dry vermouth**

**¹/₂ oz Campari**

**Orange peel, for garnish**

Shake whiskey, dry vermouth, and Campari over ice and strain into chilled cocktail glass. Garnish with orange peel. *Makes 1.*

*Though no relation to Harry's Bar in Venice, Harry's New York Bar attracted similarly glamorous and noteworthy patrons, such as Rita Hayworth, Humphrey Bogart, Coco Chanel—and of course, notorious 20th century barfly Ernest Hemingway.*

# RUSTY NAIL

*A perfect pairing of Scotch whisky liqueur and the very whisky it's made from. We like to add a little more scotch than Drambuie, but feel free to experiment with the ratio.*

*—created by Paul Knorr*

---

**3 parts Scotch whisky**

**1 part Drambuie**

Shake Scotch whisky and Drambuie with ice and strain over ice in a glass or pour into your flask using a funnel. If serving over ice, garnish with a wedge of lemon. *Makes 1.*

# ROB ROY

*The Rob Roy is, essentially, a Manhattan for those who prefer Scotch. Made with just whiskey, vermouth, and bitters, the Rob Roy swaps out rye whiskey (or bourbon) in favor of the smoky flavor of Scotch. The Rob Roy hasn't gained quite the same level of popularity as its rye-based contemporary, but it is no less delicious for it. As with many cocktails, your stance on the matter likely comes down to personal preference.*

—Shane Carley

---

**2 oz Scotch whisky**

**1 oz sweet vermouth**

**2 drops bitters**

**1 maraschino cherry, for garnish**

(1) Fill a mixing glass with ice and add Scotch whisky, sweet vermouth, and bitters. Stir gently to avoid clouding the drink.

(2) Add a maraschino cherry to your cocktail glass and strain the drink over it. Enjoy! *Makes 1.*

# ROB ROY IN A FLASK

*A paired down version of the Rob Roy—perfect to imbibe on the go.*
*—created by Paul Knorr*

**2 parts Scotch whisky**

**1 part sweet vermouth**

Shake Scotch whisky and sweet vermouth with ice and strain over ice in a glass or pour into your flask using a funnel. If serving over ice, garnish with a cherry. *Makes 1.*

# SELECT AND STAVE

*Sweet, smoky, and citrus flavors balance one another perfectly in this Jack Daniel's creation.*

*—courtesy of Jack Daniel's*

---

1 part Jack Daniel's
Single Barrel Select

³/₄ part sweet vermouth

³/₄ part cherry liqueur,
such as Cherry Heering

1 part fresh squeezed
orange juice

Shake whiskey, vermouth, and Cherry Heering over ice and strain into chilled martini glass with orange juice. *Makes 1.*

# SPITFIRE

*This bold, sweet flask cocktail has a real kick.*

*—created by Paul Knorr*

1 part whiskey

1 part dark rum

1 part cherry vodka

Shake whiskey, dark rum, and cherry vodka with ice and strain into a glass or pour into your flask using a funnel. *Makes 1.*

# GENTLEMAN'S MANHATTAN

*This variation on the Manhattan swaps out the traditional rye whiskey for the smoother Gentleman Jack.*

—*courtesy of Jack Daniel's*

---

**2 parts Gentleman Jack**

**½ part sweet vermouth**

**½ part dry vermouth**

**2 dashes of bitters**

**Cherry or lemon twist, for garnish**

Shake whiskey, sweet vermouth, dry vermouth, and bitters, and strain into chilled cocktail glass. Garnish with cherry or lemon twist. *Makes 1.*

# GODFATHER

*Named for the 1970s classic film, this drink is said to have been a favorite of Marlon Brando's.*

*—created by Paul Knorr*

**2 parts Scotch whisky**

**1 part amaretto**

Shake Scotch whisky and amaretto with ice and strain over ice in a rocks glass or pour into your flask using a funnel. *Makes 1.*

*Traditionally made with Scotch, this cocktail is also delicious when made with bourbon.*

# DEAL BREAKER

*A touch of absinthe gives this cocktail an inventive and unexpected twist.*
*—courtesy of Corsair Distillery*

---

**2 oz Corsair Quinoa Whiskey**

**½ oz honey**

**2 dashes Peychaud's bitters**

**1 splash absinthe**

**1 dash rhubarb bitters**

**Orange rind or wedge, for garnish**

In a mixing glass, stir to combine whiskey, honey, and Peychaud's. Strain into a small jar or rocks glass rinsed with absinthe and rhubarb bitters. No ice. Garnish with orange rind. *Makes 1.*

**CORSAIR**

**YEMAGEDDON**

**AMERICAN RYE WHISKEY**
DISTILLED FROM MALTED RYE & CHOCOLATE RYE
61.1 % ALC/VOL (122.5 PROOF)

**CORSAIR**
*SINGLE BARREL*
**GREEN MALT**

**AMERICAN MALT WHISKEY**
POT DISTILLED FROM 100% CORSAIR GREEN MALT

 %ALC/VOL  PROOF

# CORSAIR DISTILLERY

*By Carlo DeVito*

From the moment you step into a tasting room at Corsair Distillery and see the labels on the bottle, you know there is something different about the place. The three men in black-and-white suits look straight out of Quentin Tarantino's iconic *Reservoir Dogs*. They stride confidently toward you, as if they were about to walk right off the bottle, providing a hint of the place's bold attitude.

Of all the impressive whiskey makers in Tennessee and Kentucky, few compare to Corsair. Corsair is a mad whiskey scientist's dream. In one visit we tasted almost a dozen different whiskeys. Everything from nine-grain bourbon to quinoa whiskey to two types of hopped whiskey. Even the most dyed-in-the-wool curmudgeons grudgingly admit that this is one of the most interesting distilleries in the entire U.S. No matter what anyone says, the entire Kentucky and Tennessee community has one eye fixed on Corsair.

Established by Andrew Webber, Darek Bell, and Amy Lee Bell, Corsair opened its first tasting room and distillery in Bowling Green, Kentucky in 2008. In 2010 they opened their first Nashville location, now a "Brewstillery," in Marathon Village, and in 2016 opened a second location on Merrit Ave, which also serves as company headquarters.

Each location has its own distiller. Aaron Marcum is the head distiller at the Bowling Green location. Colton Weinstein is the head distiller at the Marathon location, and Clay Smith is the head distiller at the headquarters on Merritt. Each distiller makes a special number of recipes. Some are very specific, and particular to one person. Sometimes whiskeys from one part of the Corsair empire are blended with those produced at another location. Each distillery makes something unique and different, and all of them also make things that will be blended elsewhere.

One of the really important things to know is that while Corsair has a reputation for experimentation and small production, their three facilities make their whiskeys much easier to find than ever before. Ryemaggedon, Triple Smoke, Quinoa Whiskey, and Oatrage can be found in discerning shops, or at least ordered by your local purveyor.

# GOLDDIGGER

*Spicy and aromatic, whiskey and cinnamon schnapps make a perfect pair.*

*—created by Paul Knorr*

---

**1 part whiskey**

**1 part Goldschläger**

Shake whiskey and Goldschläger with ice and strain into a rocks glass or pour into your flask using a funnel. *Makes 1.*

# IRISH COFFEE

*The perfect wake-up cocktail and a favorite drink of airport bar patrons (or maybe that's just me). Irish Coffee is made a variety of different ways, with some including Irish Cream, some not, some specifying Irish whiskey, some not. But it just doesn't feel like "Irish" Coffee without Jameson and Bailey's, does it?*

*—Shane Carley*

---

3 parts coffee

1 dash sugar

1 part Jameson Irish whiskey

1 part Bailey's Irish Cream

Whipped cream, for garnish

(1) Pour the coffee into your glass or mug and add sugar.
Stir until the sugar has dissolved.

(2) Add whiskey and stir again.

(3) Top up with Irish cream. If you can, layer the cream on top rather than stirring it in.

(4) If desired, garnish with a dollop of whipped cream on top and enjoy!
*Makes 1.*

# JAVA JACK SHOT

*This sweet, strong concoction is great as either a shot or sipper.*
—*courtesy of Jack Daniel's*

---

**1 part Jack Daniel's Old No. 7 Tennessee Whiskey**

**1 part coffee liqueur**

Combine whiskey and coffee liqueur in a chilled shot or cocktail glass. *Makes 1.*

# HOT TODDY

*Whiskey is the perfect liquor choice for autumn or winter because it lends itself so well to warm drinks. While you could simply spike a mug of warm apple cider or add a dose to your hot chocolate, the Hot Toddy is a classic cocktail passed down through the ages. With a more well-rounded flavor than those simple suggestions, this classic is sure to warm you up quickly after a long day of snowshoeing. Customize this winter favorite with a little added mint flavor!*

—Shane Carley

---

1 part honey

2 mint leaves

4 parts tea

2 parts whiskey

Lemon juice to taste

(1) Add the honey to your mug or heat-proof glass, allowing it time to spread across the bottom. Muddle the mint leaves into it.

(2) Boil some water and make a serving of your favorite tea. Set aside.

(3) Add the whiskey and lemon juice to your drink. Use as much lemon as you might typically take with your tea.

(4) Top up the drink with the tea you set aside earlier. Gently stir, and enjoy. *Makes 1.*

# HOT TENNESSEE TODDY

*Another great warmer for anyone feeling the winter chill, Jack Daniel's soothing and slightly spiced take on the hot toddy will cure what ails you.*

*—courtesy of Jack Daniel's*

---

**1 part Jack Daniel's Old No. 7**

**1 spoonful of honey**

**1 cinnamon stick**

**1 good squeeze of fresh lemon juice**

**Hot water**

Pour whiskey into a heavy mug. Add cinnamon stick, and lemon juice. Top with hot water and stir. *Makes 1.*

"Never delay kissing a pretty girl
or opening a bottle of whiskey."

—*Ernest Hemingway*

# BOURBON

Named "America's Native Spirit" by Congress in 1964, bourbon is truly America's signature whiskey, and deeply intertwined with the history of its birthplace, Kentucky. Corn was a favorite crop of Kentucky's early pioneers, many of whom were Scottish and Scots-Irish immigrants.

Having brought the distillation techniques of their homeland with them, it was only a matter of time before they applied them to Kentucky corn. A 51%–80% corn mash bill is now enshrined as one of bourbon's defining features, which is what makes it notably sweeter than most whiskeys. Furthermore, bourbon must be aged in new, charred oak barrels, lending the spirit a smokiness, as well as notes of caramel and vanilla.

Smooth and full of flavor, bourbon works as beautifully in spirit-forward cocktails as it does in lighter drinks.

Look ahead for several spins on the best-loved bourbon cocktail of all, the Mint Julep. Now the signature drink of the Kentucky Derby, the Mint Julep was once sipped by Southern farmers as a healthful morning pick-me-up.

With tons more cocktails from both the old and new school to choose from, you'll be spoiled for choice.

# SOUTHERN CHARM

*This refreshing cucumber and watermelon cooler is just the thing to sip over hot southern summers.*

*—created by Colleen McCarthy-Clarke, courtesy of Four Roses*

---

**Three 1-by-1-inch cubes of watermelon**

**2 oz Four Roses Bourbon**

**1 oz Monin Watermelon Syrup**

**4–5 drops of Bitterman's Hopped Grapefruit Bitters**

**½ oz pomegranate liqueur, such as Pama**

**½ oz lime juice**

**8 mint leaves, plus more for garnish**

**3 cucumber half moons**

**1 oz Mr. Q's Cucumber Soda**

In a shaker tin, muddle watermelon cubes and pour off the excess juice. Add bourbon, watermelon syrup, pomegranate liqueur, bitters, lime juice, and mint leaves. Shake and double strain into a glass over crushed ice. Muddle cucumber slices in a separate dry tin with cucumber soda. Shake and double strain to top up the cocktail. Garnish with another sprig of mint. *Makes 1.*

# BUFFALO BOWTIE

*A simple but delicious twist on a Highball!*

*—created by Fran Turner of Keeneland Race Track, Lexington, Kentucky, courtesy of Buffalo Trace*

---

**1¹/₂ oz Buffalo Trace Bourbon**

**1 oz peach syrup**

**Ginger ale**

**Lime curl or bow tie, for garnish.**

Combine bourbon and peach syrup over ice in a highball glass. Top up with ginger ale and garnish with a lime curl or bow tie. *Makes 1.*

# POMEGRANATE SMASH

*Though pomegranate and bourbon may seem like an unexpected combination, these two really make a great pairing.*

*—courtesy of Maker's Mark*

---

2 parts Maker's 46 Bourbon

1 part POM Wonderful pomegranate juice

½ part honey

½ part fresh squeezed lemon juice

Pomegranate seeds, for garnish

Pour bourbon, pomegranate syrup, honey, and lemon juice into a shaker filled with ice. Shake vigorously for 10 seconds. Pour over ice into a rocks glass, and garnish with pomegranate seeds. *Makes 1.*

# PUNCH 415

*This punch takes its name from U.S. police code 415—disturbing the peace. Definitely the cocktail to have on hand for big, raucous celebrations.*

*—courtesy of Four Roses*

---

1½ oz Four Roses
Single Barrel Bourbon

¾ oz fresh lime juice

½ oz Monin orgeat syrup

2 oz pineapple juice

5 dashes Angostura bitters

Fresh mint

Combine bourbon, lime juice, orgeat syrup, pineapple juice, and bitters in a shaker. Shake. Strain into a rocks glass filled with fresh ice. Garnish with mint. *Makes 1.*

# FOUR ROSES DISTILLERY

*By Carlo DeVito*

It is said that when Paul Jones Jr., the founder of Four Roses, wrote to propose to his future wife, she replied that if her answer were "Yes," she would wear a corsage of roses on her gown to the upcoming ball. Lo and behold, she did, and in doing so inspired the name of Four Roses Bourbon. Jones registered the name in 1888, and the Spanish Mission-style distillery in Lawrenceburg was erected between 1908 and 1910, and is listed on the National Register of Historic Places.

Although it was the best-selling Kentucky bourbon in the U.S. throughout the 1930s, 1940s, and 1950s, it was purchased by Seagram, which later decided to halt domestic sales and market Four Roses exclusively to international markets. Although the brand was hugely popular abroad, especially in Asia, it was not available in the states for more than two generations. Fortunately, after Four Roses was sold to Kirin, the brand was swiftly returned to the U.S. market, largely thanks to the lobbying of former Master Distiller Jim Rutledge. It is now back in its rightful place among the country's top whiskeys.

Four Roses uses two mash bills that are mixed and matched with five yeast strains to produce their Kentucky bourbon. That makes for 10 different bourbons. The standard "Yellow Label" is made from an even blend of all 10.

Four Roses Master Distiller Brent Elliott is probably one of the most promising in the entire region. He is taking on a project few distillers ever get the chance to, and using this opportunity to create some spectacular bourbons. His single-barrel releases and his meticulous attention to recipes and pairings reveal the promise to become one of the great distillers of all-time. In other words, Four Roses is back!

Four Roses.
Four Roses
125
Small Batch
2013 Release
BARREL
STRENGTH
KENTUCKY STRAIGHT BOURBON WHISKEY

# MASON JAR BOURBON PRESS

*A classic cocktail for whiskey lovers, the Bourbon Press is a perfect drink for anytime and anywhere. It's very much an outdoor drink, right down to its appearance: It looks like nothing so much as a glass of lemonade or iced tea. In this case, a drop or two of orange bitters will add a little bit of a twist to this classic flavor combo. The Bourbon Press is the perfect drink to take to the park while you relax with a good book. Screw a lid on that Mason jar and head out there!*

—Shane Carley

---

2 oz bourbon

1 dash orange bitters

2 oz ginger ale

2 oz club soda

Mint, for garnish

Slice of lemon, for garnish

(1) Add a few good-sized ice cubes to your Mason jar and pour in bourbon and orange bitters.

(2) Top up the remainder of the glass with equal parts ginger ale and club soda.

(3) Garnish with mint and a slice of lemon and enjoy. *Makes 1.*

# WHALEN SMASH

*Whiskey and ginger is a time-honored flavor combination, but precious few whiskey cocktails do an adequate job including mint. The Whalen Smash forgoes the ginger liqueurs that similar cocktails often call for, instead adding a splash of ginger ale to give the drink some added lightness. The carbonation gives the drink a playful element, but doesn't overwhelm the palate, leaving plenty of room for the mint and lemon to play off one another.*

—Shane Carley

---

½ lemon, cut into thirds, plus more lemon or lime slices, for garnish

4 mint leaves

3 parts bourbon

1 part ginger beer

(1) Squeeze juice from lemon wedges into your glass or julep cup. Drop in the squeezed wedges.

(2) Add mint and muddle to combine with lemon juice. Add ice as desired.

(3) Pour in bourbon, then top up with a splash of ginger beer. Gently stir. Garnish with citrus and enjoy! *Makes 1.*

# THUNDER PUNCH

*Taking its inspiration from the Fuzzy Navel and the Moscow Mule, Thunder Punch strikes the perfect balance of sweet and sour.*

—*created at Drakes, Louisville, Kentucky, courtesy of Four Roses*

---

Lemon wheels

1½ oz Four Roses Yellow Label Bourbon

½ oz Finest Call peach purée

½ oz Stirrings blood orange cocktail bitters

¼ oz Finest Call lemon juice

1½ oz Regatta ginger beer, for topping up

Place lemon wheels in the bottom of a Hurricane glass. Fill with ice. Add bourbon, peach purée, blood orange bitters, and lemon juice to a shaker tin with ice. Shake for 10 seconds. Strain over ice into Hurricane glass. Add lemon wheels to glass. Top with ginger beer. *Makes 1.*

# BOURBON WHISKEY SOUR

*Delicious, a total breeze to make and great for entertaining, the sour is a classic for good reason.*

*—courtesy of Hartfield & Co.*

---

2 oz Hartfield & Co. Bourbon Whiskey

³/₄ oz simple syrup (1:1 sugar to water ratio)

³/₄ oz fresh lemon juice

1 egg white

1 lemon peel, for garnish

(1) Build whiskey, simple syrup, lemon juice, and egg white in a shaker, and dry shake (a shake without ice)

(2) Add ice and shake again. Double strain into double rocks glass over fresh ice. Express oil from lemon peel over top, stand lemon peel in the glass, and serve. *Makes 1.*

# SUMMER CITRUS

*Honeyed citrus with a hint of bitters makes this cocktail an excellent pick-me-up after a long day in the sun.*

*—courtesy of Four Roses*

---

1¼ oz Four Roses Yellow Label Bourbon

¾ oz clover honey simple syrup (equal parts honey mixed with water)

½ oz lemon juice

½ oz grapefruit juice

Dash of Angostura bitters (or to taste)

Lemon twist, for garnish

Combine bourbon, honey simple syrup, lemon juice, grapefruit juice, and bitters in cocktail shaker. Shake. Strain onto fresh ice and garnish with lemon twist. *Makes 1.*

# WHISKEY SUNSET

*Whiskey is far from the easiest liquor to use in a summer sipper, but with a little white wine to take the edge off, the Whiskey Sunset succeeds admirably. The Whiskey Sunset incorporates a few extra sweet and sour notes to create a delicious and well-rounded concoction.*

—Shane Carley

---

**2 oz bourbon**

**2 oz white wine**

**1 oz lemonade**

**1 dash simple syrup**

**3 oz ginger ale**

**1 lemon wheel, for garnish**

(1) Fill your glass with ice. Add bourbon, white wine, lemonade, and simple syrup. Stir thoroughly, then top up with ginger ale.

(2) Garnish with a lemon wheel (feel free to add some extra citrus wheels inside the drink itself) and enjoy! *Makes 1.*

# FOUR ROSES COLLINS

*The original, gin-based Tom Collins rocketed to fame in the late 19th century—so much so that it inspired the name of the Collins glass. This 1959 incarnation from Four Roses isn't quite as old, but cements the Collins cocktail as one of the greats.*

*—courtesy of Four Roses*

---

1½ oz Four Roses Bourbon

Juice of 1 lemon

1 teaspoon sugar

Club soda

Lemon slice, for garnish

Cherries, for garnish

(1) Pour a jigger of bourbon into a tall glass over cubed ice. Add the juice of one lemon, followed by sugar.

(2) Top up with club soda and stir. Garnish with slice of lemon and cherries. Sip lovingly. *Makes 1.*

# DERBY SEASON

*Rosé and bourbon might seem like something of an odd coupling, but as with any good cocktail, it's all about getting the proportions right— try it! We promise you won't regret it.*

*—courtesy of Jim Beam*

---

**2 parts Jim Beam Black Bourbon**

**¾ parts lemon juice**

**¾ parts simple syrup**

**½ parts dry rosé**

**Lemon peel, for garnish**

Stir bourbon, lemon juice, and simple syrup in a mixing glass. Pour over ice and top up with rosé. Garnish with a lemon peel. *Makes 1.*

# SILVER 75

*This bourbon rendition of the French 75 takes its name from The Silver Dollar, a honky tonk joint in downtown Louisville, named one of the best whiskey bars by both GQ and Thrillist.*

*—created at The Silver Dollar, Louisville, Kentucky, courtesy of Four Roses*

³/₄ oz Four Roses Bourbon

¹/₂ oz simple syrup

¹/₂ oz lemon juice

About 4 oz sparkling wine

Lemon peel, for garnish

Combine bourbon, lemon, and simple syrup in a tin and shake very lightly. Strain into a wine glass or coupe and top with sparkling wine. Garnish with a lemon peel expressed and set on top of the cocktail. *Makes 1.*

# MAKER'S MULE

*A sweet, full-bodied bourbon like Maker's Mark is the ultimate foil for chilled-yet-fiery ginger beer.*

*—courtesy of Maker's Mark*

---

1½ parts Maker's Mark Bourbon

Lime juice

Cold ginger beer

Lime for garnish

In tall glass, add cubed ice. Pour in bourbon, add splash of lime juice, and top up with ginger beer. Garnish with a lime. *Makes 1.*

## HONEY SYRUP

1:1 ratio of honey and water. Bring
water to a boil. Stir in honey and lower
temperature. Continue to stir until
desired consistency.

# BUFFALO SMASH

*Strictly speaking, every smash is a julep, but a julep isn't always a smash (much like all bourbon is whiskey, but the opposite isn't necessarily true). The key difference is that a smash can use herbs other than mint, and usually brings lemon and seasonal fruit into the mix—in this case, ripe blackberries.*

*—created by Michael Harper of Old Bourbon County Kitchen in Lexington, Kentucky, courtesy of Buffalo Trace*

2 blackberries, plus more for garnish

6–8 mint leaves, plus more for garnish

1 part honey syrup

2 part lemon juice

6 parts Buffalo Trace Bourbon

Soda water, to finish

"Smash" (muddle) 2 blackberries and 6–8 mint leaves with honey syrup in shaker tin. Add lemon juice and bourbon to shaker tin. Shake vigorously with cracked ice. Double-strain into a cocktail glass with fresh crushed ice. Top up with soda water and garnish with blackberry and mint spear. *Makes 1.*

# CLASSIC MINT JULEP

*Who doesn't love a Mint Julep? The classic drink of the Kentucky Derby, the Mint Julep has remained popular with whiskey drinkers for over 100 years. With a mid-range, drinkable bourbon and a little powdered sugar (the powdered sugar is important if you want to do it right), this is a cocktail sure to see many new converts after just one taste.*

—Shane Carley

---

4 mint leaves

1 tsp powdered sugar

1 splash water

2 oz Maker's Mark Bourbon

1 mint sprig, for garnish

(1) Tear the mint leaves in half to release their flavor, then muddle them in the bottom of your glass with powdered sugar and water.

(2) Fill the glass with cracked ice, then add the bourbon. Stir gently.

(3) Garnish with a sprig of mint and enjoy! *Makes 1.*

# PERFECT MINT JULEP

*Why not take the Mint Julep to a bit more of a high-end place? If you truly appreciate subtle flavor and nuance (and are willing to spend a bit extra on the best bourbon), you can make your Mint Julep into a truly transcendent drinking experience. Be sure you drink it out of a silver or pewter cup—if you're going to call something "perfect," you'd better go all the way. The Perfect Mint Julep does just that.*

—Shane Carley

---

4 mint leaves

1 tsp powdered sugar

1 splash water

2 oz Woodford Reserve
  Bourbon

1 mint sprig, for garnish

(1) Muddle the mint leaves in the bottom of the cup with powdered sugar and water.

(2) Fill the cup with cracked ice, then add your bourbon. Stir until the outside of your cup is visibly chilled.

(3) Garnish with a sprig of mint and enjoy! *Makes 1.*

# WOODFORD RESERVE

*By Carlo DeVito*

Woodford Reserve is a sophisticated bourbon. Its flavor profile highlights brandy, cognac, and fruit. Its quotient of rye keeps it from being cloyingly sweet, making for a dryer bourbon without sacrificing its Kentucky heritage.

What makes Woodford Reserve so special? It begins with the approach of the famed distillery. The narrow, single-lane roads that lead to the company's impressive entry gate wind through some of the most beautiful horse farms in all of Kentucky.

The distillery where Woodford Reserve stands now actually began its operational life in 1780, as the Old Oscar Pepper Distillery (which later morphed into the Labrot & Graham Distillery). The seemingly ancient buildings that house Woodford Reserve today, located near the town of Versailles in north-central Kentucky, were built in 1838, technically making Woodford one of the nine oldest distilleries in operation in Kentucky today. The distillery was listed on the National Register of Historic Places in 1995, and was later designated a National Historic Landmark in 2000. Knowing that it had plenty to show off, Woodford was the first distillery to start offering tours.

According to Master Distiller Chris Morris, Woodford didn't actually make a profit for 14 years. Fortunately, money was no object. Established by Brown-Forman (owners of the famed Jack Daniel's), the small distillery has transformed from a bunch of old, dilapidated buildings into one of the nation's premiere bourbon distilleries. It was Brown-Forman's long-range thinking that sought to establish Woodford Reserve as one of the premiere distilleries in the world, on par with the best of Scotland. The storied Lincoln Henderson was Woodford's first Master Distiller, who guided the company's first decade of production and releases before handing the reins over to Morris, his protégé, in 2003.

But its beauty is not just superficial. It is one of the hardest working distilleries in the region. As one tours the many buildings, there is no question Henderson and Morris designed their distillery to reflect the best of the classic Scottish style. The old stone buildings house giant fermentation tanks made from oak and banded in wrought iron. Their spirit safe is an authentic 19th century Scottish apparatus! Everything is done by hand, the old-fashioned way.

# TWISTED JULEP

*Extra-aged Jim Beam Black, peach nectar, and brown sugar add a little more moxie to this twist on the Mint Julep.*

*—courtesy of Jim Beam*

1 sprig mint, plus more for garnish

Touch of brown sugar

Blueberries, reserving some for garnish

2 parts Jim Beam Black Bourbon

½ parts peach nectar

In a Mint Julep cup or double old-fashioned glass, muddle the mint and brown sugar. Add the blueberries and muddle again. Add crushed ice, bourbon, and peach nectar. Stir to distribute mint. Top with crushed ice. Garnish with leftover blueberries and a mint sprig. *Makes 1.*

# BLACKBERRY SAGE JULEP

*Sage and blackberry make such a great combination, especially in a julep—one really enhances the flavor of the other.*

*—courtesy of Four Roses*

---

2 blackberries, plus 3 more for garnish

2 sage sprigs, plus more for garnish

½ oz turbinado or demerara syrup (1:1 recipe or less if using a 2 parts sugar syrup)

2 oz Four Roses Small Batch Bourbon

Lightly muddle two blackberries in a shaker tin and add one sage sprig. Add syrup and bourbon and shake lightly, for just long enough to mix the ingredients together. Fine strain into a glass or julep tin, and cover with crushed ice to create a small snow cone over the top of the tin. Garnish with the remaining blackberries and sage. Serve with straws. *Makes 1.*

# KENTUCKY MAID

*The Kentucky Maid was created to celebrate the opening of SIDEBAR at Whiskey Row in 2013, which coincided with the Kentucky Derby. Naturally, it takes its inspiration from the traditional Derby Cocktail, the Mint Julep.*

*—created by Lissa Ramos, General Manager of SIDEBAR at Whiskey Row, courtesy of Buffalo Trace*

---

**2 muddled English cucumber slices, plus 1 fresh slice for garnish**

**2 oz Buffalo Trace Bourbon**

**6 fresh mint leaves, plus 1 for garnish**

**³/₄ oz fresh lime juice**

**³/₄ oz simple syrup**

Combine muddled cucumber, bourbon, mint, lime juice, and simple syrup in a cocktail shaker. Shake with ice and double strain into a glass over fresh ice. Garnish with a slice of cucumber with a sprig of mint stuck right through it. *Makes 1.*

# BOURBON SWEET TEA

*Bourbon is a favorite drink of the South, and so is sweet tea. What could be more natural than adding them together to create a refreshing and delicious beverage perfect for beating the heat?*

—*Shane Carley*

---

½ lemon, juiced

1 part bourbon

4 parts sweet tea

4 lemon wheels, for garnish

(1) Squeeze the juice from ½ lemon into a pitcher. Add the juiced portion to the pitcher.

(2) Add ice, then pour in the bourbon and sweet tea. Stir until thoroughly mixed.

(3) Pour into individual glasses and garnish each with a lemon wheel. Enjoy! *Makes 1.*

# FAMILY MEAL

*This cocktail is the ultimate afternoon pick-me-up, with cold brew concentrate adding a real kick of flavor and caffeine. Although it can be made with any cola, we love Mexican Coke (it's made with real cane sugar).*

*—created by Chef Newman Miller, Star Hill Provisions at Maker's Mark Distillery*

---

¼ part Cold Brew Coffee Concentrate (Chef Newman uses Harden coffee, which is roasted 15 miles from the distillery.)

1½ parts Maker's Mark Bourbon

Mexican Coke, as needed

Lemon peel, for garnish

Build cold-brew coffee and bourbon in a rocks or highball glass. Add ice and stir gently. Top up with Mexican Coke and squeeze oil from a strip of lemon peel over top for garnish. *Makes 1.*

# MAKER'S MARK DISTILLERY

*By Carlo DeVito*

To visit Maker's Mark is like visiting Anheuser-Busch in St. Louis. It is a blend of old and new, of high-tech and incredibly antique means.

The Maker's Mark brand was born in 1958. Five years beforehand, T. William "Bill" Samuels Sr. purchased Burks' Distillery, which was built in 1889. The distinctive square bottle was designed by Bill Sr.'s wife, Marjorie "Margie" Samuels, who also named the whiskey and developed its unique, hand-dipped red wax seal.

Notably, Maker's is among only a handful of U.S. producers who use the traditional English spelling "whisky" on their labels, each of which is printed in-house on an antique printing press. It is perhaps no surprise that Maker's Mark was the first distillery in the U.S. to be designated a National Historic Landmark while still in active production.

Master Distiller Greg Davis is the brand's best ambassador. A big man with a laugh to match, he preaches the gospel of Maker's Mark with a big smile on his face. Davis is someone who seems to work well with everyone from lab technicians to the maintenance crew.

There is no question that the level of detail put into the whiskey is nothing shy of intense. Maker's Mark positions itself as a small batch bourbon, claiming, "A bourbon that is produced/distilled in small quantities of approximately 1,000 gallons or less (20 barrels) from a mash bill of around 200 bushels of grain." Maker's Mark concentrates on three core products. Their main bourbon is referred to in-house as a "Red Top." Then there is the Cask-Strength Bourbon, and Maker's Mark 46, a bourbon that is extra-aged with French oak.

# BOURBON BENDER

*A little like a sour in a flask, this cocktail is great for summer picnics.*
—*created by Paul Knorr*

---

1 part bourbon

1 part amaretto

1 part fresh lime juice

Shake bourbon, amaretto, and lime juice with ice and strain into a glass or pour into your flask using a funnel. *Makes 1.*

# AUTUMN LEAVES

*This aromatic, spirit-forward cocktail is just the thing to warm up cool autumn evenings.*

*—created by Susie Hoyt, courtesy of Four Roses*

---

1¼ oz Four Roses
Single Bourbon

¼ oz Carpano Antica

½ oz Ramazzotti Amaro

1 dash of Angostura bitters

Lemon peel, for garnish

Pour bourbon, Carpano Antica, Ramazzotti Amaro, and bitters into a mixing glass and stir. Pour into a double old-fashioned glass over fresh ice. Garnish with a light squeeze of lemon oil and discard the peel. *Makes 1.*

# HEARTS ON FIRE

*At once earthy, fruity, and spicy, this bold cocktail definitely leaves an impression.*

*—created by Dani McQuarrie of Belle's, Lexington, Kentucky, courtesy of Buffalo Trace*

---

2 oz Buffalo Trace Bourbon

¾ oz Chambord

½ oz maraschino liqueur

2 dashes Hellfire bitters

1 edible flower, optional, for garnish

2 brandy-soaked cherries, for garnish

Pour bourbon, Chambord, maraschino liqueur, and bitters into a cocktail glass and stir. Garnish with an edible flower and two brandy-soaked cherries. *Makes 1.*

# A DARK ART

*Sophisticated, striking and sure to impress anyone you make it for, A Dark Art pairs Maker's 46 with the nutty caramel flavor of black sesame orgeat.*

—*created by Christian Villalta of Root and Square Root courtesy of Maker's Mark*

---

1½ parts Maker's 46 Bourbon

½ part black sesame orgeat

Juice of 1 lime

13 dashes Angostura bitters

Pinch of activated charcoal

Jasmine flower, optional garnish

Combine bourbon, orgeat, lime, bitters, and activated charcoal in a shaker with ice; strain into a coupe over ice and add jasmine flower for garnish. *Makes 1.*

---

# BLACK SESAME ORGEAT

½ cup black sesame seeds

2 cups hot water

3 cups sugar

½ teaspoon orange flower water

2 tablespoons vodka

(1) Toast sesame seeds for 1–2 minutes over medium heat. Let cool.

(2) In a bowl, stir together hot water and sugar until dissolved.

(3) Combine syrup and sesame seeds in a blender or food processor and blend for 1–2 minutes. Let steep for 3–12 hours.

(4) Strain the mixture through 2–3 layers of cheesecloth, squeezing as you go. Discard ground sesame seeds or set aside for later use.

(5) Add orange flower water and vodka. Bottle the syrup, which will keep for about 2 weeks.

# RISIN' OUTLAW

*This cross between an Old-Fashioned and a Manhattan is dangerously good.*
*—created by Susie Hoyt, courtesy of Four Roses*

---

1 oz Four Roses Single
Barrel Bourbon

1 oz Vida mezcal

½ oz Cocchi Americano

½ oz Dolin dry vermouth

⅛ oz demerara syrup

⅛ oz water

7 drops orange bitters

Lemon peel, for garnish
(Sazerac style)

Build and stir in an old-fashioned; add borubon, mezcal, Cocchi Americano, dry vermouth, demerara syrup, water and orange bitters. Gently stir with a barspoon. Garnish very lightly with lemon oil and discard the peel. *Makes 1.*

*This cocktail is not made or served with ice—it should be served at room temperature.*

# A COWBOY'S BREAKFAST

*This smoky-sweet drink was created for the Stampede, a massive rodeo and festival held every July in Calgary, Alberta.*

*—created by Bar C, Calgary, Alberta, courtesy of Buffalo Trace*

1½ oz Buffalo Trace Bourbon

½ oz Cazadores tequila

½ oz bacon-infused maple syrup

1 egg white

3 shakes cherry bark bitters

2 shakes liquid smoke

Candied bacon, for garnish

Dry shake the bourbon, tequila, bacon-infused maple syrup, egg white, cherry bark bitters, and liquid smoke, then shake in the ice. Garnish with candied bacon. *Makes 1.*

# BACON-INFUSED MAPLE SYRUP

½ cup maple syrup

½ cup crispy cooked bacon, chopped

Combine syrup and bacon and allow to infuse for at least one hour. Strain to remove bacon and pour syrup into a bottle or jar. *Makes about ½ cup.*

---

# CANDIED BACON

⅓ cup brown sugar

8–10 slices of bacon

1 tablespoon maple syrup, if desired

(1) Preheat oven to 400°F. Combine syrup and brown sugar in a bowl. Dredge each slice of bacon in the mixture, making sure each side is evenly covered.

(2) Bake in oven for 15–20 minutes, flipping halfway through. Remove from oven and set aside to cool until ready to serve. *Makes 8–10 slices.*

# BLACK DOG

*This Manhattan-adjacent cocktail swaps out bitters for blackberry brandy.*
*—created by Paul Knorr*

---

**3 parts bourbon**

**1 part sweet vermouth**

**1 part blackberry brandy**

Shake bourbon, sweet vermouth, and blackberry brandy with ice and strain into a glass or pour into your flask using a funnel. *Makes 1.*

# FOUR ROSES SKYSCRAPER

*According to some cocktail lore, the Skyscraper was invented by an artist who loved Manhattans. Wanting something a little lighter to drink during the day, she turned it into a tall drink by topping it off with ginger ale. This 1959 recipe from Four Roses keeps things from getting too sugary by using soda water instead.*

—*courtesy of Four Roses*

---

**3 parts Four Roses Bourbon**

**1 part sweet vermouth**

**Soda water**

Fill shaker with cracked ice, and jigger in bourbon and sweet vermouth, three parts to one. Stir until cold, pour into ice filled glass, and add soda. A real taste triumph every time! *Makes 1.*

# MAKER'S BOULEVARDIER

*Rich, sweet Maker's Mark bourbon makes for one heck of a Boulevardier.*
*—courtesy of Maker's Mark*

---

1½ parts Maker's Mark Bourbon

¾ part sweet vermouth, such as Cinzano.

¾ part Campari or Aperol

Maraschino cherry, for garnish

Stir bourbon, sweet vermouth, and Campari or Aperol with ice, strain, garnish with a cherry, and serve. *Makes 1.*

# BLACK MANHATTAN

*The addition of black walnut bitters adds a smoky twist to this bourbon Manhattan.*

*—courtesy of Four Roses*

---

1½ oz of Four Roses
Small Batch Bourbon

1 oz sweet vermouth,
preferably Carpano Antica

2–3 dash black walnut bitters

Maraschino cherry

Add bourbon, vermouth, bitters, and ice to mixing glass, and stir until glass is frosted. Use strainer to separate ice and cocktail into chilled martini glass (neat). Add cherry. Stir. *Makes 1.*

# SPRING MANHATTAN

*This springtime spin on a Manhattan lightens things up a little with the addition of aperitif wine.*

*—courtesy of Jim Beam*

---

**2 parts Jim Beam Black Bourbon**

**½ parts aperitif wine**

**½ parts sweet vermouth**

Stir bourbon, aperitif wine, and sweet vermouth with ice in a mixing glass. Strain into a chilled cocktail glass. *Makes 1.*

# MAKER'S MARK MANHATTAN

*A slight variation on the classic Manhattan, with the bold, complex flavor of Maker's Mark 46, aged in seared French oak staves.*

—*courtesy of Maker's Mark*

---

2 parts Maker's 46 Bourbon

½ part sweet vermouth

1–2 dashes Angostura bitters

Maraschino cherries, for garnish

Pour bourbon, sweet vermouth, and bitters into a mixing glass with ice cubes. Stir well. Strain into a chilled cocktail glass. Garnish with cherries. *Makes 1.*

# CLASSIC OLD-FASHIONED

*It's hard to anoint a "favorite" whiskey cocktail, but the Old-Fashioned certainly challenges for the spot. Featuring just sugar, bitters, and a little bit of citrus to accent the flavor of the whiskey, the Old-Fashioned is a sophisticated drink for the seasoned whiskey drinker. For the Classic version of the cocktail, an underrated, extremely drinkable whiskey like Maker's Mark will serve your purposes perfectly.*

—*Shane Carley*

---

**1 splash simple syrup**

**1 strip orange rind**

**2 drops bitters**

**2 oz Maker's Mark Bourbon**

**1 maraschino cherry, for garnish**

(1) Add simple syrup to an old-fashioned glass and drop in a slice of orange rind. Add bitters and muddle together.

(2) Fill the glass with ice, then add bourbon.
Stir together slowly.

(3) Garnish with a maraschino cherry and enjoy! *Makes 1.*

# HEAVEN HILL DISTILLERIES

*By Carlo DeVito*

Heaven Hill Distilleries, located in Bardstown, Kentucky, is recognized by whiskey lovers the world over as an American treasure, home to impressive names such as Evan Williams and Elijah Craig.

To give you just a measure of how amazing this place is, you need to understand that Heaven Hill is the seventh-largest seller of spirits in America. Heaven Hill also warehouses the second-largest cache of bourbon whiskey in the world. The distillery has 54 rickhouses in all. Heaven Hill is also the largest independent family-owned and -operated distiller and seller of spirits in the United States. And to top it off, of all the liquor giants, it is the only large, completely family-owned distillery headquartered in Kentucky!

Heaven Hill was established in 1935 by a group of investors which included famed distiller Joseph L. Beam (first cousin of Jim Beam), a member of the Shapira family, and several others. Over the intervening years, the Shapira brothers slowly bought out the other investors. The five brothers, Ed, Gary, George, David, and Mose Shapira were a tightly knit group who gathered every Sunday at their mother's house with their families. As the children played, the men reviewed last week's events, and planned out the next week. Since then, Heaven Hill has remained under the ownership of the Shapiras, with a Beam as Master Distiller until only recently.

Of all the brands in the Heaven Hill portfolio, none is bigger than Evan Williams. It is one of the world's best-selling bourbons. This bourbon is named after Welsh immigrant Evan Williams, who came across the Atlantic and in 1783 settled in an area now known as Louisville. He founded Kentucky's first commercial distillery, an achievement now commemorated with a plaque. Although some whiskey historians have challenged the veracity of these claims, nothing concrete has ever been produced to name another claimant.

# PERFECT OLD-FASHIONED

*For the Perfect Old-Fashioned, eschew the simple syrup in favor of a sugar cube and some water, and rely on the garnishes for the small punch of citrus that the drink requires. Using a top-shelf whiskey like Woodford Reserve will enhance the drinkability of the cocktail, while still keeping you in a reasonably accessible price range. Sure, you could spend hundreds of dollars on bourbon. But if you do that, you probably aren't watering it down with a cocktail, no matter how delicious it may be.*

—*Shane Carley*

---

1 sugar cube

2 drops bitters

1 splash water

2 oz Woodford Reserve Bourbon

1 orange slice, for garnish

1 maraschino cherry, for garnish

(1) Put sugar cube into a rocks glass, and saturate it with bitters. Add a small splash of water and muddle.

(2) Fill the glass with ice and add bourbon. Stir lightly.

(3) Garnish with a slice of orange and a maraschino cherry and enjoy! *Makes 1.*

# THE O.G. O.F.

*Full of warm spices and notes of caramel from the demerara syrup, this aromatic Old-Fashioned cocktail is best enjoyed on chilly winter nights.*

*—created by Pam Wiznitzer, USBG NY President and Creative Director at Seamstress, NYC, courtesy of Maker's Mark*

---

**2 parts Maker's Mark Cask Strength Bourbon**

**¼ parts Cocktail & Sons Spiced demerara syrup**

**2 dashes Angostura bitters**

**2 dashes Bittermans ole bitters**

**Flamed orange twist, for garnish**

Stir bourbon, demerara syrup, and both kinds of bitters with ice and strain into chilled glass. Garnish with a flamed orange twist. *Makes 1.*

*Freeze orange slices into ice cubes and add to cocktail a fun seasonal twist.*

**CORSAIR**
## GRAINIAC
### 9 GRAIN BOURBON
46% ALC/VOL (92 PROOF)

TENNESSEE BOURBON
⅑ DISTILLED FROM CORN, BARLEY, RYE, WHEAT
OATS, QUINOA, TRITICALE, SPELT AND BUCKWHEAT

# FASHIONABLY OLD

*Corsair's Grainiac incorporates oat, buckwheat, triticale, spelt, and quinoa into the standard bourbon mash bill. A surprising and complex bourbon, it makes for a nutty, earthy take on the Old-Fashioned.*

*—courtesy of Corsair Distillery*

---

2 oz Corsair Grainiac
9 Grain Bourbon

¼ oz Demerara sugar

3 dashes barrel-aged bitters

Orange zest (or lemon twist),
for garnish

Combine bourbon, demerara sugar, and bitters in a mixing glass with cracked ice. Stir for 30–45 seconds. Strain into a rocks glass with fresh ice. Garnish with orange zest. *Makes 1.*

# MISH MASH

*Ever forget to restock your liquor cabinet for a few weeks, or maybe even months? Once in a while, you open the cabinet and realize you're left with just a handful of odds and ends that don't really make anything. The Mish Mash takes a couple of odds and ends that you should always have a half bottle of or so, mixes in a bit of bourbon, and gives you a surprisingly delicious result.*

—*Shane Carley*

---

2 parts bourbon whiskey

1 part triple sec

1 part simple syrup

1 splash grenadine

Lemon peel, for garnish
(if desired)

(1) Fill a glass with ice and add bourbon, triple sec, and simple syrup.

(2) Stir together until mixed. Top with a splash of grenadine and if desired, a lemon peel. Enjoy! *Makes 1.*

# SEAHORSE

*The name of this large batch cocktail is inspired by our Old Bardstown Bottled in Bond Bourbon, which was named for a famous racehorse of the same name from Calumet Farm in Lexington, Kentucky. I have an obsession with all things mermaid, and we originally had thought of naming the drink Mermaid Morning. However, after deciding to use Old Bardstown (and sampling the cocktail!) we determined that Seahorse was a much more fitting name.*

—*Britt Kulsveen Chavanne of Willett Distillery*

1750 ml bottle of Old Bardstown Bottled In Bond, Kentucky Straight Bourbon

1 gallon of orange juice, preferably non-organic; in this drink, organic orange juice can taste quite medicinal.

One 16 oz bottle of Santa Cruz organic pure lemon juice

1 full cap of blood orange bitters, preferably Stirrings

One 8 oz cup of simple syrup, preferably Sugar in the Raw

Thick slices of star fruit generously pre-soaked in Noah's Mill Small Batch Bourbon, for garnish

Luxardo cherries and Luxardo syrup, for garnish

Combine bourbon, orange juice, lemon juice, bitters, and simple syrup in a large punch bowl. Chill in refrigerator. Garnish each drink with a slice of star fruit, Luxardo cherries, and a drizzle of Luxardo syrup. *Serves a crowd.*

# FOUR ROSES
# SPICED PUNCH

*Bowl over the crowd at your holiday party with this refreshing and festive chai-spiced punch.*

*—courtesy of Four Roses*

---

6 lemons, plus 1 for garnish

1 cup granulated sugar

4 cups water

8 chai tea bags

1 cup Four Roses Bourbon

1 can (12 oz) ginger beer

Assorted cinnamon sticks, cloves, star anise, and allspice, for garnish

(1) Peel six lemons with potato peeler and set naked lemons aside. Put lemon peels and sugar in a bowl; crush peels into sugar. Let sit for 1 hour.

(2) Juice the naked lemons and strain juice to remove pulp.

(3) Brew eight chai tea bags in water. Discard bags after use. Dissolve sugar and lemon peel mixture in chai tea while warm. Remove peels and discard. Add bourbon and lemon juice. Chill in refrigerator.

(4) Before serving, top up with ginger beer. Garnish with lemon wheels and assorted spices floating in punch. *Serves a crowd.*

# OLD-FASHIONED EGGNOG

*This recipe yields 5 pints of the grandest Eggnog ever ladled into a cup. An original Four Roses creation, this recipe dates all the way back to 1936!*

—*courtesy of Four Roses*

---

6 eggs

³/₄ cup sugar, divided

1 pint cream

1 pint milk

1 pint Four Roses Bourbon

1 oz Jamaican rum

Grated nutmeg, for garnish

(1) Beat the yolks and whites of six eggs separately. Add ½ cup of sugar to the yolks while beating. Add ¼ cup of sugar to whites after beating until very stiff.

(2) Mix egg whites with yolks, and stir in one pint of cream and one pint of milk. Add a pint of bourbon and 1 oz of rum, and stir thoroughly.

(3) Serve cold with grated nutmeg. *Serves a crowd.*

# FOUR ROSES HOT TODDY

*Another delicious seasonal cocktail, Four Roses created this winter warmer way back in 1943.*

*—courtesy of Four Roses*

---

1 cube of sugar

Hot water

Lemon

1½ oz Four Roses Bourbon

4 cloves

1 stick cinnamon

Place a cube of sugar in the bottom of a mug or hot toddy glass and dissolve with a little hot water. Add twist of lemon peel (bruise firmly), cloves and, if you desire, a stick of cinnamon. Pour a generous jigger of bourbon into your mug. Fill the glass with steaming hot water. Enjoy! *Makes 1.*

# HOT BUTTERED BOURBON

*This rich bourbon variation of Hot Buttered Rum is going to be your new wintertime favorite.*

*—created at El Camino, Louisville, Kentucky, courtesy of Four Roses*

---

Very hot water

1 oz (or 1 heaping dessert spoon) Hot Buttered Rum Mix

1½ oz Four Roses Bourbon

1 dash Angostura bitters

Grated nutmeg or tall cinnamon stick, for garnish

Fill mug up to the top with hot water and allow to temper for 45 seconds. Dump hot water and refill to ⅔ with hot water. Add a heaping dessert spoon of Hot Buttered Rum mix and stir vigorously. Add bourbon and bitters. Top up with more hot water if needed and give a quick stir. Garnish with grated nutmeg or a tall cinnamon stick, or both, and serve with the spoon in. *Makes 1.*

---

# HOT BUTTERED RUM MIX

1 lb butter at room temperature

6 cups brown sugar

4 teaspoon cinnamon

2 teaspoon grated nutmeg (fresh)

1 teaspoon ground cloves

1 teaspoon salt

Combine and stir until evenly mixed. *Makes about 6 cups.*

# HOT APPLE CIDER

*This recipe for spiked cider makes enough for 15 servings, and has the added benefit of filling your home with the gorgeous scent of spices, apple and orange.*

*—courtesy of Four Roses*

---

**1 liter Four Roses Yellow Label Bourbon**

**2 liters apple cider**

**5 cinnamon sticks**

**3 oranges, for garnish**

**30–40 cloves**

Put bourbon and the apple cider in an electric cooking pot or on the stove on low for two hours before guests arrive. Add cinnamon sticks, making sure that the liquid is not boiling (this can bring out bitter/woody notes from the cinnamon). Peel 3-by-1-inch sections of the oranges, and garnish each cocktail with a clove-studded orange peel. *Serves a crowd.*

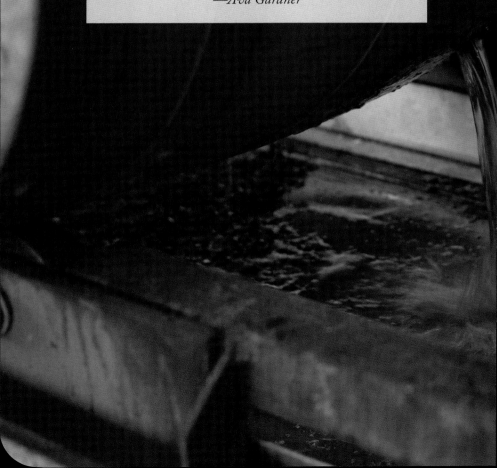

I wish to live to 150 years old,  but the day
I die, I wish it to be with  a cigarette in one
hand and a glass of  whiskey in the other.

—*Ava Gardner*

# RYE

Like bourbon, rye is an entirely American invention. Once popular throughout the northeastern United States and even distilled by George Washington himself, rye whiskey was almost wiped out by the Prohibition. Long eclipsed by other whiskeys, rye has recently enjoyed a renaissance, with more and more distilleries capitalizing on its popularity every year.

Although its flavor profile varies somewhat from label to label, rye whiskey's minimum 51% rye grain mash bill makes it a dryer, spicier whiskey, lending a bold, peppery quality to any drink.

Of all the rye cocktails, the most famous by far is the Manhattan. Although its exact origins are disputed, we know that the Manhattan first appeared in New York City in the late 19th century, and that it quickly took the world by storm. Although the post-Prohibition years have seen Manhattans made with bourbon and Canadian whisky, rye's resurgence has seen the original return to its rightful place on cocktail menus across the globe.

Rye's spicy yet smooth finish works well in any number of mixed drinks. In the following pages, you'll find zippy interpretations of sour, smash, and swizzle cocktails, as well as more quintessential rye cocktails, like the Sazerac and Vieux Carré. Enjoy!

# RYE SOUR

*Ah yes, the famous Whiskey Sour. Made a variety of different ways, sometimes with egg whites, sometimes with sour mix, and sometimes simply made with lemon juice. The drink is as sour as its name implies, adding an unexpected new dimension to the whiskey. The Whiskey Sour takes whiskey and lemon juice and smashes them together head on, creating this delicious, classic concoction.*

—Shane Carley

---

2¹/₂ oz rye whiskey

1 oz lemon juice

¹/₃ oz simple syrup

1 maraschino cherry, for garnish

1 lemon slice, for garnish

(1) Add rye whiskey, lemon juice, and simple syrup to a shaker with ice. Shake vigorously.

(2) Strain the resulting mixture into a glass over ice.

(3) Garnish with a maraschino cherry and a slice of lemon and enjoy! *Makes 1.*

# BUDGET RYE SOUR

*One of the great things about living in the modern age is the convenience. There are microwave dinners, there is juice in a pouch, and anyone who doesn't feel like mixing a cocktail can go out and buy a mix to make their lives easier. As far as mixes go, sour mix is probably one of the more popular options and makes the Budget Sour a convenient, hassle-free alternative to the traditional Whiskey Sour.*

—Shane Carley

---

1 part rye whiskey

2 parts sour mix

1 lemon slice, for garnish

(1) Add whiskey and sour mix to a sour glass over ice. Stir until thoroughly mixed.

(2) Garnish with a lemon slice and enjoy! *Makes 1.*

# FALCON SMASH

*Sweet basil and Corsair's peppery Ryemageddon make an ace combination in this Smash cocktail.*

*—courtesy of Corsair Distillery*

---

**2 oz Corsair Ryemageddon Whiskey**

**1 oz lemon juice**

**6 basil leaves, plus more for garnish**

**1 oz simple syrup**

Combine rye whiskey, lemon juice, basil leaves, and simple syrup in a rocks glass. Gently muddle basil and top with ice. Garnish with one or two additional leaves. *Makes 1.*

# WATER FOR ELEPHANTS RYE SWIZZLE

*A classic Swizzle is a lot like a sour style cocktail, but mixed with a swizzle stick and served in a tall glass with lots of ice. Originally from the Caribbean and often made with rum, it's the ultimate summer cocktail. Willett's Rye Swizzle benefits from the herbal, honeyed flavor of their Family Estate Small Batch Rye, with Tippleman's Double Falernum Syrup supplying an extra kick of ginger, clove, and lime zest.*

*—courtesy of Willett Distillery*

---

**1–2 oz Willett Family Estate Small Batch Rye, Cask Strength**

**Juice from one whole lime, freshly squeezed**

**3–4 shakes bitters of your choice**

**1 oz Tippleman's Double Falernum syrup**

Combine rye, lime juice, bitters, and syrup in Collins glass. Top with ice and swizzle. *Makes 1.*

# WILLETT DISTILLERY

*By Carlo DeVito*

Willett Distillery can be found just outside Bardstown, Kentucky. The site, which was once the family farm, is also home to Kentucky Bourbon Distillers (aka KBD). Both businesses have been held and run by the Willett family for generations. They are makers and bottlers of bourbon and rye under the Willett flagship name, as well as a slew of other labels. Their whiskeys range from two to 27 years in age.

According to the distillery, John David Willett was born on December 26, 1841 in Nelson County, Kentucky. He was one-third owner and Master Distiller at Moore, Willett & Frenke Distillery. During his lifetime, John David was also the Master Distiller at four other distilleries in Kentucky. Aloysius Lambert Willett, who went by Lambert, was born September 23, 1883 in Bardstown. Lambert was in the Kentucky bourbon business from the age of 15, and served several distilleries across the commonwealth in various capacities. His son, Aloysius Lambert Thompson Willett, would be the founder of the Willett Distillery in Bardstown.

Willett Distilling used grandfather John's bourbon recipes as a blueprint to create the whiskey that they would make into Old Bardstown. They made 30 barrels on March 17, 1937. By 1960, they had filled their 100,000th barrel. Over the first 20 years or so, the distillery introduced several new labels including Old Bardstown and Johnny Drum. However, the distillery fell on hard times and was shuttered by 1980.

Under Martha and Even Kulsveen, Thompson's daughter and son-in-law, the distillery evolved into KBD, becoming "the big daddy of bourbon and rye bottling." The family reintroduced the Willett name as a brand in 2012, and now produces a dizzying array of small labels.

A very extensive rebuilding and expansion transformed Willett immensely. Today, Master Distiller Drew Kulsveen oversees an operation that has three stills, including a column still with a doubler and a beautiful pot still. There are eight smallish warehouses on the original distillery grounds, which hold approximately 40–48,000 barrels in total.

# WAX AND WANE

*Basil, rosemary, and charred cedar lend a woodsy, herbal note to this sophisticated interpretation of a Whiskey Sour.*

*—courtesy of Corsair Distillery*

---

2 oz Corsair's
Ryemageddon Whiskey

¼ oz fresh squeezed
lemon juice

¼ oz Demerara
simple syrup

4 dashes Angostora bitters

1 egg white

6 basil leaves

1 sprig of rosemary, for garnish

1 cedar paper by Fire and Flavor,
for garnish

Put rye whiskey, lemon juice, demerara simple syrup, bitters, egg white, and basil leaves into a shaker, followed by ice. Shake, and double strain into a tall Collins glass over ice. Briefly (and carefully!) catch the cedar paper on fire, extinguish it, then add to it your drink with the rosemary sprig. *Makes 1.*

# CLASSIC MANHATTAN

*Whiskey and vermouth is a classic combination, and one with which it's difficult to go wrong. The Manhattan makes use of this simple combination and, with the addition of just a few drops of bitters, creates something truly fantastic. A refined and elegant cocktail, the Classic Manhattan offers the everyday mixologist a simple way to enjoy an old classic.*

—Shane Carley

---

**2 oz Knob Creek Rye Whiskey**

**²/₃ oz sweet vermouth**

**2 drops bitters**

**Cherries, for garnish**

(1) Fill a mixing glass with ice and add rye whiskey, sweet vermouth, and bitters. Stir gently to avoid clouding the drink.

(2) Strain the resulting mixture into a cocktail glass.

(3) Garnish with a cherry or two and enjoy! *Makes 1.*

# JIM BEAM DISTILLERY

*By Carlo DeVito*

If there is a first family of bourbon, it is the Beam family. There are no less than three or four distilleries that boast a Beam family connection. The name and the family have been synonymous with bourbon for more than 200 years.

"The first Boehm in Kentucky was Johannes Jacob Boehm, who arrived in Kentucky in 1787 or 1788. He preferred to be called Jacob Boehm and later Jacob Beam," wrote Frank Prial in the New York Times. Jacob had been a farmer, and sold his first barrels of corn whiskey sometime around 1795. The whiskey more or less resembled the bourbon we drink today. His distillery came to be known as Old Tub, and the whiskey came to be known as Old Jake Beam sour mash.

Under Jacob's son and grandson, David Beam and David M. Beam, the business expanded its distribution by leaps and bounds, eventually relocating the distillery to Nelson County, which had increased access to railroads. In turn, the Jim Beam brand's namesake, James Beauregard Beam, went on to rebuild the distillery once more in 1933, this time in Clermont, Kentucky, where it remains today. The brand officially became known as "Jim Beam Bourbon" in 1935, with James's son, T. Jeremiah Beam, as Master Distiller. Remarkably, with the sole exception of Jerry Dalton, every Master Distiller in Jim Beam's history has been a direct descendant of Jacob Beam. Jim Beam's grandson, Frederick Booker Noe II, known simply as Booker Noe, was Master Distiller at the Jim Beam Distillery for more than 40 years, and his son, Fred Noe, is the current Master Distiller.

Jim Beam produces an average of approximately 300,000 barrels per year. Most of the barrels are new American white oak No. 4 Char, which is also known as alligator skin. The distillery has 22 fermenters that produce 45,000 gallons each of distiller's beer, and the column still is six stories high. Most of their rickhouses hold up to 60,000 barrels each!

Among Beam's illustrious and extensive lineup of bourbons, including the bold Jim Beam Black and a number of successful flavored and spiced bourbons, is the Small Batch Bourbon Collection. This portfolio of craft-styled bourbons includes prestigious, limited-edition brands such as Knob Creek, Booker's, Basil Hayden's, and Baker's.

# SHANE'S PERFECT MANHATTAN

*When it comes to a cocktail as classy as the Manhattan, why settle for anything less than the finest ingredients? By building your drink around top-shelf whiskey, you can be sure that you're getting the best tasting Manhattan around. The Perfect Manhattan is made using Whistlepig Straight Rye Whiskey, one of the most delicious whiskeys the average person can get their hands on.*

*—Shane Carley*

---

**2 oz Whistlepig Straight Rye Whiskey**

**²/₃ oz sweet vermouth**

**2 drops bitters**

**1 maraschino cherry, for garnish**

(1) Fill a mixing glass with ice and add rye whiskey, sweet vermouth, and bitters. Stir gently to avoid clouding the drink.

(2) Put a maraschino cherry in the bottom of a glass and strain the liquid ingredients over it. Enjoy! *Makes 1.*

# TEMPTATION

*Floral and citrus flavors combine with a hint of that signature rye spice to make this tempting, spirit-forward cocktail.*

*—created by Paul Knorr*

---

**2 parts rye whiskey**

**1 part Dubonnet Blonde**

**1 part triple sec**

**1 part Pernod**

Put rye whiskey, Dubonnet Blonde, triple sec, and Pernod into a shaker. Shake with ice and strain over ice in a rocks glass or pour into your flask using a funnel. *Makes 1.*

# THOMPSON'S OLD-FASHIONED

*Supremely versatile, the Old-Fashioned formula works with just about any whiskey—and indeed, almost any spirit. Named for Thompson Willett, founder of the original Willett Distillery, this Old-Fashioned gets a kick from Willett's Family Estate Rye, but is equally good when made with their Pure Kentucky Small Batch or Noah's Mill Bourbons. We encourage you to try them all.*

*—courtesy of Willett Distillery*

---

1 teaspoon simple syrup

3–4 shakes of bitters (your choice)

2 oz Willett Family Estate Rye (or Willett Pure Kentucky Small Batch Bourbon or Noah's Mill Bourbon.)

Water or club soda, if desired

Luxardo cherries, for garnish

Orange peel, for garnish

Combine simple syrup and bitters in a tumbler. Top with ice and fill with rye. Leave a little room for water or club soda if desired. Drop in one or two Luxardo cherries and rub the orange peel around the rim of the glass. Do not share! *Makes 1.*

# PREAKNESS

*Bénédictine gives this Manhattan-inspired flask cocktail a sweet, herbal twist.*
*—created by Paul Knorr*

---

**4 parts rye**

**1 part Bénédictine**

**1 part sweet vermouth**

**4 dashes Angostura bitters**

Combine rye, Bénédictine, sweet vermouth, and bitters in a shaker. Shake with ice and strain into a glass or pour into your flask using a funnel. *Makes 1.*

# VIEUX CARRÉ

*One of the Big Easy's many contributions to cocktail history, the Vieux Carré was created by head bartender Walter Bergeron at the Hotel Monteleone in 1938. This complex sipping cocktail, which uses two types of bitters, evokes the languorous decadence of New Orleans.*

*—courtesy of Jack Daniel's*

---

¾ parts Jack Daniel's Tennessee Rye

¾ parts cognac

¾ Noilly Prat Rouge vermouth

¼ teaspoon Bénédictine

2 dashes Peychaud's bitters

2 dashes Angostura bitters

Combine rye whiskey, cognac, vermouth, Bénédictine, and both kinds of bitters in a rocks glass, add ice, stir, and serve. *Makes 1.*

# FRISCO

*A simple and oft-overlooked cocktail that predates the Prohibition, the Frisco mellows the bite of rye whiskey with aromatic and slightly syrupy Bénédictine.*

—*created by Paul Knorr*

---

**2 parts rye**

**1 part lemon juice**

**Splash Bénédictine**

Shake rye, lemon juice, and Bénédictine with ice and strain over ice in a glass or pour into your flask using a funnel. *Makes 1.*

# SAZERAC

*The official cocktail of New Orleans—originated in Antoine Peychaud's apothecary on Rue Royal in the 1830s. Since then, it has evolved into the harmonious blend of bitters, anise, and rye that we know today.*

*—courtesy of Jack Daniel's*

---

1½ oz Jack Daniel's
Single Barrel Rye

2 dashes Peychaud's bitters

1 dash Angostura bitters

1 bar spoon absinthe

1 lemon peel, for garnish

Build rye whiskey, bitters, and absinthe a rocks glass. Garnish with a lemon peel. *Makes 1.*

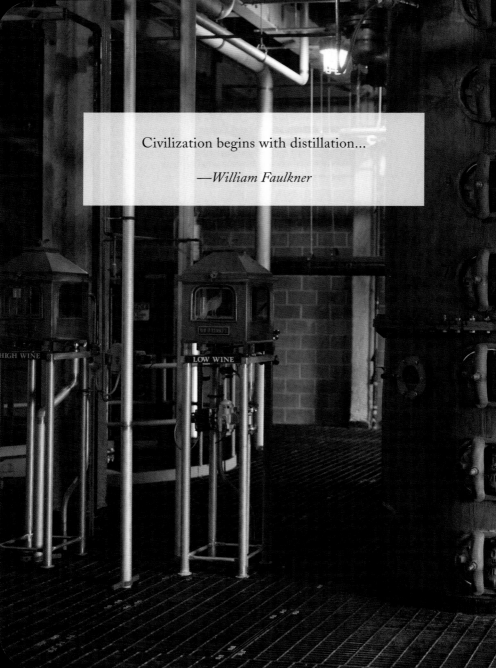

Civilization begins with distillation...

—*William Faulkner*

# SWEETER STUFF: WHISKEY LIQUEURS AND CREAMS

Over the past few years, whiskey liqueurs and creams have become something of a party favorite, but they are much more than a drink for the college crowd or those with a serious sweet tooth. In fact, the oldest whiskey in the world is a bottle of Glenavon Special liqueur whisky, believed to have been bottled sometime between 1851 and 1858 by the Glenavon Distillery in Ballindalloch, Scotland.

Many of the major distilleries have at least one or two types of whiskey liqueur, often flavored with additional ingredients that complement the whiskey's flavor, like honey, vanilla, apple, and spices.

Sweet and aromatic, whiskey liqueurs are ideal for sipping after dinner and are more versatile in mixed drinks than you might think. Using a whiskey liqueur as the base for your cocktail doesn't have to make it a syrupy confection—you could actually argue that it's a great simplifier, omitting any need for simple syrup or sugar.

In this chapter, you'll find crisp and refreshing concoctions, rich and indulgent cocktails that double as desserts, as well as fiery, spiced drinks that will alight the senses. Take your pick!

# MILA'S SIGNATURE COCKTAIL

*Developed by whiskey lover and Jim Beam brand ambassador Mila Kunis, this refreshing cocktail is the perfect balance of sweet vanilla and tart grapefruit.*

*—courtesy of Jim Beam*

---

**1 part Jim Beam Vanilla**

**2 parts fresh grapefruit juice**

**1 part club soda**

**Grapefruit slice, for garnish**

Combine vanilla whiskey, grapefruit juice, and club soda over ice and and stir. Garnish with grapefruit slice. *Makes 1.*

# SUMMER HONEY

*Refreshing and full of summer fruit flavor, this is the ideal drink to sip while lying poolside.*

—*courtesy of Jack Daniel's*

---

1 part Jack Daniel's Tennessee Honey

1/2 part Midori

1 part pineapple juice

3 parts lemon-lime soda

Orange slice, for garnish

Combine honey whiskey, Midori, and pineapple juice in shaker with ice. Shake, add lemon-lime soda, and serve in a rocks glass. Garnish with orange slice. *Makes 1.*

# KENTUCKY VANILLA DROP

*This simple twist on the classic Lemon Drop cocktail balances tart lemon with creamy vanilla—a little like a lemon creamsicle. Enjoy as a shot or sipping cocktail.*

*—courtesy of Jim Beam*

---

1 part Jim Beam Vanilla

1 part lemon sour

Combine vanilla whiskey and lemon sour in a shaker with ice. Shake and strain into a chilled shot or cocktail glass. *Makes 1.*

# VANILLA SMASH

*Warm vanilla, cool mint, and a generous helping of lemon make this summertime cocktail a smash hit.*

—*courtesy of Jim Beam*

---

2 lemon wedges

6–8 mint leaves

1 part Jim Beam Vanilla

Muddle mint and lemon in a double old-fashioned glass. Fill with ice and add vanilla whiskey. *Makes 1.*

# JACK HONEY
# AND LEMONADE

*Crisp, tangy lemonade partners perfectly with Jack Daniel's Tennessee Honey.*
*—courtesy of Jack Daniel's*

---

1½ parts Jack Daniel's
Tennessee Honey

6–8 parts lemonade

Mint leaves, for garnish

Build honey whiskey and lemonade over ice and stir. Garnish with mint. *Makes 1.*

# JACK HONEY AND TEA

*The ultimate Southern duo: sweet tea and Jack Daniel's. Simple enough to throw together at the end of a long day, delicious enough to serve as a big batch party cocktail.*

—*courtesy of Jack Daniel's*

---

**1½ parts Jack Daniel's Tennessee Honey**

**6–8 parts tea**

**Mint, for garnish**

Build honey whiskey and tea over ice and stir. Garnish with mint. *Makes 1.*

# SIGNATURE SERVE

*Jim Beam Vanilla enhances the classic bourbon and coke cocktail.*

*—courtesy of Jim Beam*

---

**1 part Jim Beam Vanilla**

**2 parts cola**

**Cherry, for garnish**

Build vanilla whiskey and cola over ice and stir. Garnish with cherry. *Makes 1.*

# BOURBON BALL MILKSHAKE

*This seriously rich and indulgent spiked milkshake marries smooth bourbon cream with ice cream, fudge, and candied pecans. Decadence in a glass.*

*—created by Lissa Ramos and the staff of SIDEBAR at Whiskey Row, courtesy of Buffalo Trace*

---

4 scoops vanilla bean ice cream

2 oz Buffalo Trace Bourbon Bourbon Cream Liquor

2 oz chocolate fudge

Chocolate syrup

Whipped cream

Candied pecans, for garnish (if desired)

Combine ice cream, bourbon cream liquor, and chocolate fudge in a blender. Decorate the inside of a frozen glass with drizzles of chocolate syrup. Pour milkshake into the chocolate syrup-lined glass and top with whipped cream, more chocolate syrup, and candied pecans, if desired. *Makes 1.*

# BUFFALO TRACE DISTILLERY

*By Carlo DeVito*

When you first get to Buffalo Trace, you are instantly overwhelmed by the size of the place. It almost resembles a steel mill more than it resembles a distillery. One of the largest distilleries in the region, it is also the oldest continually operating distillery in the United States, and a designated National Historic Landmark.

To walk around the distillery is to step back in time. The stairs are well worn, the walls are smooth from wear, and parts of the operation have the look of 19th century industry. But it's not marketing—it's authentic. Located in Frankfort, Kentucky, the distillery is situated on what is believed to be the site of a centuries-old buffalo crossing. Another name for where American bison trails cross is a trace, giving the distillery its distinctive name.

Yet this is but one of many names the distillery has operated under. Records show that Hancock Lee and his brother Willis Lee first began distilling on this spot in 1775. Commodore Richard Taylor constructed the first building on the site in 1792, Riverside House, which still stands today. Harrison Blanton built the first full distillery in 1812, and Edmund H. Taylor bought the distillery in 1870. Taylor named the distillery the Old Fire Copper (O.F.C.) Distillery. George T. Stagg bought the distillery, along with the Old Oscar Pepper Distillery, eight years later. Stagg built the first steam-fitted, climate-controlled warehouse for whiskey aging in the United States.

Today, Buffalo Trace's 17 rickhouses are chocked with barrels, and the company believes that each floor has its own terroir, its own individual and unique climate. Now owned by Sazerac and under the guidance of Master Distiller Harlen Wheatley, Buffalo Trace produces numerous bourbons and whiskeys, including such brands as Buffalo Trace, E. H. Taylor, W. L. Weller, Sazerac, Pappy Van Winkle, Rare Eagle, and George T. Stagg.

# VANILLA FIZZ

*This creamy, frothy confection is a Kentucky-style spin on the New Orleans Gin Fizz.*

*—courtesy of Jim Beam*

---

1 part Jim Beam Vanilla

2 parts half-and-half

1 part fresh lemon sour

1 part egg white

Club soda

Orange peel, for garnish

(1) Combine vanilla whiskey, half-and-half, lemon sour, and egg white in a shaker. Shake vigorously for as long as you can.

(2) Strain into a chilled Collins glass and spritz with club soda (the egg whites will grow out of the glass).

(3) Garnish with an orange peel. *Makes 1.*

# HONEYCHATA

*Full of sugar and spice, this sweet, smooth blend of rum, bourbon, cinnamon and honey is a great after dinner sipper.*

*—courtesy of Jack Daniel's*

---

1 part Jack Daniel's
Tennessee Honey

1 part Rumchata

Shake honey whiskey and Rumchata with ice and strain into a chilled shot glass or over ice in a rocks glass. *Makes 1.*

# FIRE EXTINGUISHER

*Sipped side-by-side, apple cider and Jack Daniel's fiery cinnamon liqueur make a perfect pair.*

*—courtesy of Jack Daniel's*

---

**1 shot Jack Daniel's Tennessee Fire**

**1 pint hard apple cider**

In a chilled glass, combine cinnamon whiskey and hard apple cider. *Makes 1.*

# CINNAMON APPLE

*Whether in an apple pie or an apple crumble, there are few flavors that go together more perfectly than cinnamon and apple. It might even be called the quintessential flavor of our land. After all, what's more American than apple pie? But pies are work, and they take time. Why spend the whole day preparing an apple pie when you can drink one instead? The Cinnamon Apple cocktail features the delicious flavors you expect from your favorite homemade treats, but with a delightful buzz in lieu of the sugar rush.*

—Shane Carley

---

2 parts apple cider

1 part apple liqueur

1 part cinnamon whiskey

1 cinnamon stick, for garnish

1 apple slice, for garnish

(1) Fill an old-fashioned glass with ice and add cider, apple liqueur, and cinnamon whiskey. Stir until thoroughly mixed.

(2) Garnish with a cinnamon stick and enjoy! *Makes 1.*

# GOLD FURNACE

*If you're looking to light a fire in your belly, this sweet and savory triple-spiced concoction will do the trick.*

—*created by Paul Knorr*

---

**1 part Fireball Cinnamon Whiskey**

**1 part Goldschläger**

**Tabasco sauce**

Shake cinnamon whiskey and Goldschläger with ice and strain into a shot glass or pour into your flask using a funnel. Top with Tabasco to taste. *Makes 1.*

Whisky is liquid sunshine.

—*George Bernard Shaw*

# INDEX

## A

Apple Sangria, 41
Autumn Leaves, 140

## B

Bellini, 33
Black Dog, 150
Black Forest, 42
Black Manhattan, 157
Blackberry Sage Julep, 128
Bourbon Ball Milkshake, 239
Bourbon Bender, 139
Bourbon Sweet Tea, 132
Bourbon Whiskey Sour, 104
Brown Derby, 34
Budget Rye Sour, 192
Buffalo Bowtie, 91
Buffalo Smash, 119
Buffalo Trace Distillery, 240

## C

Cactus Jack, 30
Cinnamon Apple, 248
Classic Manhattan, 203
Classic Mint Julep, 120
Classic Old-Fashioned, 162
Corsair Distillery, 73
Cowboy's Breakfast, A, 148-149

## D

Dark Art, A, 144
Dark Side, 45
Deal Breaker, 70
Derby Season, 112

## F

Falcon Smash, 195
Family Meal, 135
Fashionably Old, 171
Fire Extinguisher, 247
Four Roses Collins, 111
Four Roses Distillery, 96
Four Roses Hot Toddy, 180
Four Roses Skyscraper, 153
Four Roses Spiced Punch, 176
Frisco, 216

## G

Gentleman's Manhattan, 66
Godfather, 69
Golddigger, 74
Gold Furnace, 251

## H

Hartfield & Co. Distillery, 47
Hearts On Fire, 143
Heaven Hill Distilleries, 165
Honeychata, 244
Hot Apple Cider, 184
Hot Buttered Bourbon, 183
Hot Tennessee Toddy, 82
Hot Toddy, 81

## I

Innuendo, 13
Irish Coffee, 77
Irish Rose, 29

## J

Jack & Cola, 18
Jack & Ginger, 22
Jack Daniel's Boulevardier, 54
Jack Daniel's Distillery, 25
Jack Honey and Lemonade, 232
Jack Honey and Tea, 235
Jack Julep, 37
Java Jack Shot, 78
Jim Beam Distillery, 204

## K

Kentucky Maid, 131
Kentucky Vanilla Drop, 228

## M

Maker's Boulevardier, 154
Maker's Mark Distillery, 136
Maker's Mark Manhattan, 161
Maker's Mule, 116
Mason Jar Bourbon Press, 99
Mila's Signature Cocktail, 224
Mish Mash, 172

## O

O.G. O.F., The, 168
Old as Dirt, 53
Old-Fashioned Eggnog, 179

## P

Perfect Mint Julep, 123
Perfect Old-Fashioned, 167
Pomegranate Smash, 92
Preakness, 212
Punch 415, 95

## R

Renegade Lemonade, 38
Risin' Outlaw, 147
Rob Roy, 58
Rob Roy in a Flask, 61

Rusty Nail, 57
Rye Sour, 191

## S

Sazerac, 219
Seahorse, 175
Select and Stave, 62
Shane's Perfect Manhattan, 207
Signature Serve, 236
Silver 75, 115
Single Barrel Old-Fashioned, 50
Snake Bite, 49
South of NY Sour, 17
Southern Charm, 88
Spitfire, 65
Spring Manhattan, 158
Summer Citrus, 107
Summer Honey, 227

## T

Temptation, 208
Tennessee Mule, 26
Thompson's Old-Fashioned, 211
Thunder Punch, 103
Twisted Julep, 127

## V

Vanilla Fizz, 243
Vanilla Smash, 231
Vieux Carré, 215

## W

Water for Elephants
    Rye Swizzle, 196
Wax and Wane, 200
Whalen Smash, 100
Whiskey Nut, 21
Whiskey Sling, 14
Whiskey Sunset, 108
Willett Distillery, 199
Woodford Reserve, 124

# ABOUT WHALEN BOOK WORKS

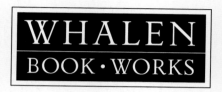

Whalen Book Works is a small, independent book publishing company based in Kennebunkport, Maine, that combines top-notch design, unique formats, and fresh content to create truly innovative gift books.

Our unconventional approach to bookmaking is a close-knit, creative, and collaborative process among authors, artists, designers, editors, and booksellers. We publish a small, carefully curated list each season, and we take the time to make each book exactly what it needs to be.

We believe in giving back. That's why we plant one tree for every ten books we sell. Your purchase supports a tree in a United States National Park.

*Get in touch!*

Visit us at **Whalenbooks.com** or write to us at 68 North Street, Kennebunkport, ME 04046.